LOPSIDED

EA KAFKALAS

ISBN: 978-1-951186-11-1 eBook

ISBN: 978-1-951186-10-4 Paperback

Published by EAK Arts, 1549 Route 20, New Lebanon, NY 12125
Printed in the United States

1

SPECIAL NOTE: ALL GROUPS RECEIVING PERMISSION TO PRODUCE *LOPSIDED* are required to give credit to the author as sole and exclusive author of the play in all programs distributed in connection with performances of the play and in all instances in which the title of the play appears for purposes of advertising, publicizing or otherwise exploiting the play and/or a production thereof; the name of the author must appear on a separate line, in which no other names appear, immediately beneath the title and in a size of type equal to 50% of the largest letter used for the title of the play. All title pages in the program books must contain the following credit: *LOPSIDED* was commissioned by Cedar Crest College and made its world premiere on 24 September 1994 in the Little Theatre, Alumnae Hall.

Dedication

*For Helen Kirchofer,
and far too many others!*

Acknowledgments

The playwright gives special thanks to: Eileen Bannon, Belka Bednar, Michele DeFrancisco, Pat Oren, Betty Winters, the American Cancer Society, the Cancer Support Team at St. Luke's Hospital (Allentown, PA), the members of Encore and Make Today Count, the Reach to Recovery Volunteers, and all the survivors of breast cancer that took the time to share their stories. The staff, cast and crew of the Cedar Crest Stage Company, her friends, family, and adopted sisters, and most particularly Helen Kirchofer. Without their love and support *LOPSIDED* would not have been written.

Original Production

LOPSIDED WAS COMMISSIONED BY CEDAR CREST COLLEGE. WHERE it premiered on 23 September 1994. The original cast was as follows:

MEGAN: Jessica Ellis
LAURIE: Robyn Puchyr
MARY: Kirsten Morabito
GAIL: Melissa Colflesh
PETER: Mark Fatzinger

Director : Steve Hatzai
Production Designer: Roxanne T. Amico
Technical Direction: Glenn Gerchman
Stage manager: Stacie Cassel
Assistant stage manager: Kris Kemmerer

Forward

LOPSIDED EXPLORES A MULTITUDE OF INTERACTIONS WE EXPERIENCE every day. The perennial subject of breast cancer is more timely today then when EA Kafkalas first wrote the play. She handles this intense subject in the only way possible: with an illimitable array of humor and passion. The key to this script is that the characters are not idealized, nor are the situations.

Surrounding the central issue of cancer are topics of life and death, marriage and friendship, trust and deception. The characters are allowed, even encouraged, to thrive within this contextual framework. The dialogue is witty albeit real. Simply stated this treatment is the most poignant I have yet to read on the subject.

—Rita Kogler Carver
Author, *Stagecraft Fundamentals*

Characters

(in order of appearance:)

MEGAN SINGER: IS A PHOTOJOURNALIST FOR *MILLENNIUM* magazine, twenty-six years old.

LAURIE KOVAK: is a high school teacher living in Gaithersburg, MD, twenty-seven years old.

MARY LEWIS: is a doctor interning at the Great Ormond Street Hospital for Children, London, England, twenty-seven years old.

GAIL WILLIAMS: is a manager at a boutique in New York City, twenty-seven years old

PETER LEWIS: is a studio musician, twenty-three years old.

A Note from the Author

I AM THRILLED YOU ARE READING THIS, WHETHER IT BE FOR PURE enjoyment or for production consideration.

LOPSIDED was commissioned by my alma mater, Cedar Crest College, in 1994. I was given the following guidelines: the play had to address breast cancer, have only one male cast member, and be able to be performed with a limited set. I had three months to research and write the piece, followed by an extensive workshop period and ultimately, the production. It was a bit daunting as I had not had cancer at that time.

I began my research by reaching out to local breast cancer support groups in Pennsylvania's Lehigh Valley where I lived at the time. I was overwhelmed by the response I received. The demographic at that time was mostly women over fifty. As a young character actor myself, I knew the challenges of playing someone older. I was also living through the beginnings of the AIDS epidemic and had already lost numerous friends to the hideous disease. The women who would be playing these parts initially were young, and many were not practicing safe sex. I hoped that having them play younger women might help them grasp the seriousness of the breast cancer threat at a younger age. Thus, I chose a younger cast.

Some of the research was heartbreaking, seeing women who were feeling "less than" after having a part of their body removed which they felt was intrinsic to their identity as a woman. My research was conducted via a survey passed out in the support groups. This allowed women to remain anonymous and helped inspire a more honest response. I rarely spoke directly with anyone, unless they indicated I could. It was at that time I made the acquaintance of Helen She was a survivor, having undergone a full mastectomy for a different type of breast cancer—one that didn't present as a lump. Her support of this project was indispensable, and she insisted that I let people know that breast cancer didn't only present in the form of a lump. She was fully supportive of the idea that one of the women had a lover who had died of her type of cancer as it was particularly insidious. All these elements led me to set the play in a reunion situation.

It was my intent that you would leave *LOPSIDED* having learned about the effects of cancer on the survivor, their friends, and their caretakers.

I am grateful to Cedar Crest College for believing in me and pushing me to write what I hope you will find is not a lecture on breast cancer but a look at what cancer can do to a group of friends. I hope you also see how a woman, who feels the loss of part of her body/identity, can face the challenge of loving again.

As pointed out, by a delightful, older gentlemen at the New York reading, in the end, *LOPSIDED* is a romantic comedy.

Enjoy!

Yours in art,

EA Kafkalas

A Note on the Staging

LOPSIDED HAS BECOME A PERIOD PIECE. COMMISSIONED AND written in 1994 before many advancements in diagnosis and treatment of breast cancer took place, it is dated. At that time a diagnosis was simply "breast cancer" and treatment was usually a lumpectomy or mastectomy followed by chemotherapy and radiation. A woman wanting reconstruction could get implants (already deemed dangerous). The advancements in handling breast cancer have come so far. For those reasons, I prefer the play be performed as a period piece.

The play runs approximately ninety minutes, and is best performed without an intermission. Should you require an intermission, it must take place between scenes six and seven.

Having seen the play performed in various spaces from a fifty, seventy-five and two-hundred-thirty seat theater, I feel it works better in an intimate setting, both in size and configuration.

The use of the unit set has been successful in all productions. Allow props, lighting, and costumes to indicate location changes to better focus on the dialogue.

Scene Breakdown

ONE:
A hotel room, Wednesday before Mary's wedding

TWO:
A pub, Wednesday evening

THREE:
A hotel room, later Wednesday evening

FOUR:
A hotel room, Thursday morning

FIVE:
Heathrow Airport, Thursday afternoon

SIX:
The garden of Paul's parents house, Thursday evening

SEVEN:
A hotel room, later Thursday evening

EIGHT:
Park bench, Friday morning

NINE:
A pub, Friday evening

TEN:
A hotel room, later Friday evening

ELEVEN:
The garden of Paul's parent's house, Saturday after Mary's wedding

*LOPSIDED is written to be performed
without intermission*

Setting

The play takes place
in London, England
June 1994

LOPSIDED

by

EA KAFKALAS

Scene One

A Wednesday afternoon before Mary's wedding. The lights come up on a hotel room. Megan enters the room. She is carrying a small suitcase and has a camera bag over her shoulder. The sound of a shower is heard. Clothes are laid out on a bed. Megan sets her things down and takes a look around the room. Laurie emerges from the bathroom in a plush hotel robe, startled to see Megan there. Megan turns to greet her.

MEGAN: Laurie. Oh, God it's so great to see you. It's been . . .

LAURIE: Three years. You were shooting a rally across the river.

(She kisses Megan on the cheek.)

MEGAN: What no hug?

LAURIE: Maybe later.

MEGAN: Afraid I'm going to rip your robe off and ravish you.

LAURIE: Not really. *(Picks up her clothes)* How's the magazine?

MEGAN: *(sits on the bed)* It's my life now. I work, I eat, and then I work some more. Mother says I'll either have a Pulitzer or a heart attack by thirty if I don't slow down, so I told her, "you're the editor, order me to slow down."

LAURIE: But you haven't, have you?

MEGAN: Since when did any of us listen to our mothers?

LAURIE: Let me finish up in the bathroom and then you can freshen up.

MEGAN: *(Sighs)* Still won't change in front of me.

LAURIE: Still paranoid as ever. I don't want to excite you too much.

MEGAN: That'll be the day.

(Laurie sits next to Megan.)

LAURIE: I'm glad that you came, Meg. I know that it means a lot to Mary to have her friends here when she's so far from home.

MEGAN: Well, I wasn't going to miss the chance to catch a glimpse of the guy that stole Mary's heart. She's had her head in her books so long; I never thought she'd meet anyone.

LAURIE: I heard she met him at a hospital fundraiser. He just swept her off her feet.

MEGAN: I just hope she's happy. That's all that matters to me.

LAURIE: She sounds like she is.

MEGAN: That's good. I just wish it took more than a wedding or a funeral to get us back together these days.

LAURIE: *(Seriously)* I'm sorry about Danielle.

MEGAN: Thanks. I got your note.

LAURIE: Let me change and then we can catch up, okay? *(Heads for the bathroom.)*

MEGAN: So have you seen the dresses? *(Turns and bumps Laurie, and Laurie's clothes tumble to the ground.)* Sorry

LAURIE: *(bends to pick up clothes. Megan helps her. Laurie tries to stop her.)* I can get them.

MEGAN: It's no trouble. So, you didn't answer my question. The dresses? Something out of *Gone with the Wind* maybe? *(She reaches for Laurie's bra. Laurie tries to grab it, but Megan already has it in her hand.)*

LAURIE: I think *even* you are going to be pleasantly surprised.

MEGAN: *(feels the prosthesis in the bra. Megan looks at it and then at Laurie)* No. Tell me this isn't yours.

LAURIE: Well we know it's not yours. *(Tries to take the bra from Megan, but Megan doesn't let go.)*

MEGAN: *(There is a silence, as Megan seems to be remembering something as she holds the bra)* When?

LAURIE: Seven months ago. Hell-of-a Christmas present, huh? *(Takes the bra from Megan and sets the clothes back on the bed.)*

MEGAN: Why didn't you tell me?

LAURIE: You're not exactly the easiest person to find.

MEGAN: You could have called the magazine. I would have come. It's not like Mother isn't giving me fluff pieces since Dannie's funeral.

LAURIE: It wasn't necessary for you to come.

MEGAN: I would have though.

LAURIE: I know. Look, Meg, Mary told me about Danielle. I know that she . . .

MEGAN: Died from it.

LAURIE: Yeah *(opens her arms)* I'll take that hug now.

(Megan hugs Laurie and doesn't let go.)

Hey, it's okay. I'm not going anywhere.

MEGAN: *(lets go)* Were you ever gonna' tell me?

LAURIE: I only told Mary, because, I was scared and I wanted someone to answer my questions, someone that gave a damn about me.

MEGAN: And I don't. You didn't think I could take it?

LAURIE: It's not a question of "taking it." Look, from what Mary told me about Dannie . . . I didn't want to burden you. It seemed like you'd been through so much, so quickly.

MEGAN: Jesus, Laurie, I'm your best friend. Were you gonna' tell me at all?

LAURIE: I don't know, Meg. Maybe I wanted to see you first. To talk about your latest assignment, my star pupils, something other than this God-damned cancer. Look, if it's any consolation, I don't think I have the same kind as Dannie. Things look pretty good for me.

MEGAN: What kind is it?

LAURIE: Intraductal Carcinoma. Which means . . .

MEGAN: It was in a duct, and it didn't spread, and you probably found a hard lump. If I'm not mistaken your odds are pretty good if you found it early enough.

LAURIE: You've done your research.

MEGAN: I read anything I could get my hands on.

(Takes Laurie's hand and they sit on the bed.)

What did you have done?

LAURIE: Mastectomy followed by radiation.

MEGAN: Why'd they do that?

LAURIE: Small boobs.

MEGAN: They sure they got it all?

LAURIE: As sure as they can be.

MEGAN: Still tired from the radiation?

LAURIE: Not as much. I did feel tired when I had the radiation, and it's not the kind of tired that sleeping helps. I was so exhausted I had to rearrange my teaching schedule though. Fortunately the school was great.

MEGAN: Dannie had inflammatory breast cancer. She didn't find a lump or anything. Her skin was red and warm for a month or so. The doctor thought it was an infection he gave her some antibiotics. When they didn't work he sent her for a biopsy. There was chemo and a double mastectomy and then more chemo . . . doesn't sound anything like yours. Dannie's was very rare. Spreads in the lymph nodes of the skin. They did everything they could, they just found it too late.

LAURIE: I'm really sorry, Meg, I know how much she meant to you.

MEGAN: I think about her all the time. I even have her diaries. Her publisher wants me to release them, says they could help other women. I've been thinking about doing it. I mean if it could help someone else. Just so people could know there are different kinds.

LAURIE: I use one of Dannie's stories in my new writers course. I just started doing it last September. I thought I'd tell her in my Christmas card . . .

MEGAN: Which one?

LAURIE: What?

MEGAN: Which story?

LAURIE: *Losing My Heart.*

MEGAN: She would have been pleased. *(Laughs)* She would have liked the irony of this.

LAURIE: I hope you don't mind, Meg but I specifically asked Mary to put us together. I couldn't be around Gail right now, and I didn't really want to be alone . . .

MEGAN: No. I'm glad I'm with you and not Gail. She didn't even acknowledge Dannie's death. So, why didn't Stu come? Senator couldn't get by without him?

LAURIE: *(stands and picks clothes up)* He's history.

(Laurie exits into the bathroom.)

MEGAN: He left you?

LAURIE: *(from offstage)* Said he couldn't take losing me. I haven't even heard from him since I began radiation. He just packed his things and left. No forwarding address or anything.

MEGAN: What an asshole. When did he leave you?

LAURIE: January, after the operation.

MEGAN: So you went through this all by yourself?

LAURIE: No. My mom came to stay with me.

MEGAN: How is your Mom?

LAURIE: She's great.

MEGAN: What about your Dad?

LAURIE: I called home to tell them about the operation, and my father answered, and I said, "Daddy, I have some disturbing news. I have to have a mastectomy." And my father said, "Uh, I think you better talk to your mother dear." and passed the phone to Mom.

MEGAN: But he came to see you, right?

LAURIE: Oh, yeah, he was there with Mom and Stuart when I woke up from surgery.

(She enters, dressed in an outfit buttoned all the way up to the top button.)

Well?

MEGAN: You always look beautiful, Laurie, you know that.

LAURIE: You always were a charmer.

(Laurie kisses Megan on the cheek.)

MEGAN: I mean it.

LAURIE: Thank you. I just have to believe it again. Come on. Freshen up and lets go to the party.

(Megan exits into the bathroom.)

MEGAN: *(from offstage)* You know Stu is a real asshole. I met a lot of great guys during Dannie's hospitalizations. Most of them were concerned about the cancer, not their wives breasts. I guess old Gail would be surprised her Prince Stuart turned out to be such a toad. I know this one woman who has the same kind of cancer as Dannie did. She was thinking about reconstruction, and her husband told her not to have it done for him. He was happy with her just the way she was. *(Emerges from the bathroom, hair combed, and a new top)* I just can't believe anyone would be dumb enough to let you go.

LAURIE: *(laughs)* You always were my biggest fan. Should we go?

MEGAN: *(motions to the door)* After you.

(Lights fade.)

Scene Two

A pub, the same Wednesday, later that evening. Mary sits at a table, dressed in a party outfit waiting. On the table sits a bottle of champagne chilling. There are four glasses. Megan and Laurie enter.

MARY: MEG, LAURIE! *(She moves to greet them)*

LAURIE: You look great, Mary *(hugs Mary)*

MARY: You look pretty good yourself.

MEGAN: I see she got a hug right off the bat. *(Hugs Mary)* And, I have a bone to pick with you, Doc.

MARY: *(looks at Laurie)* You told her?

MEGAN: I beat it out of her.

MARY: Don't look at me. She made me promise.

LAURIE: *(sits down)* Could we change the subject. Please.

MARY: How are you doing, Meg?

MEGAN: I'm doing the best I can, Doc.

MARY: Well, I'm glad you came.

MEGAN: I wouldn't have missed it for the world.

MARY: Thanks.

(Megan and Mary cross to the table to join Laurie.)

MEGAN: Are we just waiting for Gail?

LAURIE: Who else. *(Reaches for the bottle.)* Maybe we should open the champagne while we're waiting.

MEGAN: Sounds good to me.

MARY: Maybe we should wait for Gail.

MEGAN and LAURIE: Nah.

MEGAN: You know Gail. *(Looks at her watch)* She's running on Gail time. *(Starts to open and then pour the champagne)* Remember that time that you and I waited two hours for her at Eddie's restaurant? *(To Laurie)* We were supposed to meet for brunch and then go to a movie. When she finally did show up, we had eaten and were ready to go the movie . . .

MARY: Yeah, and she got pissed off at us for wanting to leave her there alone.

MEGAN: And of course you and I stood our ground and ended up seeing that awful movie. What was it?

MARY: I don't remember. All I remember is we missed the one we wanted to see while we were waiting at Eddie's.

LAURIE: Well, I say we toast. *(Raises her glass)* To Mary and Paul and marital bliss...

MEGAN: To friendship.

ALL: Here. Here.

*(They all click glasses and drink. Gail enters. She is
dressed in the latest fashion.)*

GAIL: I see you've started without me. No problem. I'll just catch up.
*(Takes a sip of champagne. Then she starts around the circle greeting
each person.)* Mary, you look divine. Megan, sorry about Dannie. I
would have written but . . .

MEGAN: You never could pick up a pen.

GAIL: And Laurie, How's Stuart?

LAURIE: I wouldn't know. I haven't seen him since January.

GAIL: Mary didn't tell me that. *(Smacks Mary on top of the head and
sits down)* So he's available?

MEGAN: Not much of a catch, if you ask me

GAIL: But he's a terrific lay, isn't he, Laurie?

LAURIE: Define terrific?

MARY: Don't start anything.

GAIL: Who me?

MEGAN: So how's the Greenwich Village boutique?

GAIL: Margarita is still a bitch. She hasn't given me a raise in over two
years, even though I've taken over most of the managerial responsibili-
ties. But my therapist tells me that I need to assert myself more and get
these hostilities out.

MEGAN: You're still seeing that therapist.

GAIL: I'm down to once a week except when I have PMS. So, Laurie,
how's the brat pack?

LAURIE: Fine.

MEGAN: So, Doc, you got us all back together for this shindig. What's the plan?

MARY: Tomorrow we go for fittings. Then we can do the sight seeing stuff. Buckingham Palace, Westminster Abbey, The Wallace Collection, and the Tower of London where the crown jewels are on display. Then tomorrow evening Paul's family is having a party at their country house. The night after we have the rehearsal and after that Paul and I have agreed we will have our own little "last night" flings with our respective friends. I thought we could go to Planet Hollywood. Then Saturday, Paul and I get married.

GAIL: Sounds simply splendid. So, Laurie, why did you dump Stuart?

LAURIE: I didn't dump him.

GAIL: Then that means he dumped you.

MARY: I'm warning you, Gail, drop it.

GAIL: Just asking questions of people I haven't seen in several years. I didn't realize that was a capital crime.

MEGAN: So when do we get to meet your fiancé?

MARY: Tomorrow at his parents' house.

GAIL: I can't wait. I'm a little surprised though, I mean I heard the English are so stiff. Or is that what you like about him?

MARY: It's good to see that some people never change.

GAIL: Well, it seems Stuart had a change of heart.

MARY: Gail!

LAURIE: *(Rises to leave)* Look, I don't have time for this shit! I thought we were all adults now.

GAIL: Don't be so dramatic...

LAURIE: I'm gonna' go upstairs and lie down.

MARY: Don't leave Laurie.

LAURIE: I'm sorry Mary. I'm feeling a little jet lagged. I just need to lie down. *(Kisses Mary on the cheek)*

MARY: I'll come check on you.

LAURIE: I'm fine. *(She exits)*

MEGAN: *(to Gail)* You just can't let anything go can you?

GAIL: Hey, she stole my fucking boyfriend, not yours!

MEGAN: She didn't steal Stuart, what is he a piece of property? Maybe he just preferred being with someone that wasn't always on the rag.

GAIL: And what the hell does that mean?

MEGAN: You know exactly what it means. *(Mary tries to stop Megan.)* Excuse me, Doc, I don't want to destroy what's left of your evening. I'm gonna' go check on Laurie.

MARY: *(to Gail)* Remind me to invite you to all my parties that I want to ruin.

(Lights fade.)

Scene Three

LAURIE AND MEGAN'S HOTEL ROOM, LATER WEDNESDAY EVENING. LAURIE has locked herself in the bathroom. Megan is sitting on the bed cleaning her camera equipment.

MEGAN: I COULD SHOW YOU SOME OF MY PHOTOGRAPHS OF THE RICH and over photographed. I brought my proofs.

LAURIE: *(from offstage)* I told you to leave me alone.

MEGAN: I'm not the one that was a shit to you. You don't have to be mean to me. I gave up a perfectly good fluff piece at Club Med to see you people, the least you could do is pretend you're happy to see me.

LAURIE: *(emerges from the bathroom.)* I'm sorry *(sits on the edge of the bed.)* You've never been a shit to me.

MEGAN: Not in several years anyway.

LAURIE: Why can't she let it go?

MEGAN: 'Cuz she's insecure. She's always been. She was on a mission at school, and you got in the way. You know she was out for her

M.R.S. degree. Jesus, don't you remember how her mother used to call her every weekend, "Are you seeing anyone? Are you going steady? Are you engaged?" The girl was on a manhunt and her mother was like a vulture waiting for the kill.

LAURIE: Sometimes, I think that God is punishing me?

MEGAN: Why would she do that?

LAURIE: I wish you'd stop calling him her. Do you have to carry everything to the extreme?

MEGAN: I don't make fun of your beliefs.

LAURIE: Well, I think he's sitting up there saying, "Laurie Kovack, you've been a shit."

MEGAN: Gail's right about one thing, you are dramatic.

LAURIE: I don't feel dramatic. I've been through so much crap in the past year. I have to have done something wrong.

MEGAN: Like what?

LAURIE: I did everything you were supposed to do, Meg. Low fat diet, alcohol only on the weekends in limited quantity, the gym three times a week . . . and I still got it.

MEGAN: But no one knows what causes it.

LAURIE: Don't you see it must have been something I did.

MEGAN: Something like dating Stuart Pompous Ass the Third?

LAURIE: Meg, I got this cough after the radiation. *(Crosses away from Megan)*. This incessant, persistent cough that haunted me wherever I went. And I thought this is it? This is worse than Chinese water torture. It's not bad enough I lost part of my body, I'm undergoing radiation to kill off mutant cells growing in my system, I feel like a truck hit me—I have this cough. Any time I went to laugh, or cry, or even breathe—I'd cough. It was maddening. And I tried to not let it get to me. I tried to keep a "good attitude." But I couldn't help but think, it's something I've done. God is punishing me for something I've done . . . And for the life of me I can't figure out what it is . . . I thought it was because I took Stuart, but then he left me.

MEGAN: *(crosses to Laurie and tries to comfort her.)* Shh, Stop beating up on yourself. No one deserves cancer.

LAURIE: I never meant to hurt Gail.

MEGAN: I know.

LAURIE: I should have known she'd want him back. She always wanted him back. But, I went out with him anyway. Why'd I do that?

MEGAN: No accounting for taste I guess.

LAURIE: I shouldn't have done it, Meg.

MEGAN: But you did, and that's not why any of this is happening. I know how you feel, or at least I know that Dannie felt the same way when they were pumping her system full of poison, I mean that's what chemotherapy is, isn't it? But it's not a punishment. God's not like that. She's all forgiving. If she's not how do you explain the little kids that get it, how rotten could they be? It just happens. And it sucks when it does, but it is not your fault.

LAURIE: I'm gonna' get ready for bed. *(Crosses to the table to get her makeup bag.)*

MEGAN: You don't believe me.

LAURIE: I can't accept that this didn't happen for a reason.

MEGAN: Why not?

LAURIE: Everything happens for a reason, Meg, that's the way things are.

MEGAN: You have to be so damn analytical about everything.

LAURIE: Staring the grim reaper in the face does that to you.

MEGAN: I don't want to talk about this with you. *(Grabs her coat and camera case.)*

LAURIE: Why not?

MEGAN: Because I need to get some air. I'm gonna' take a walk.

LAURIE: Go ahead.

MEGAN: I will. I'll catch you later.

(MEGAN exits. Lights fade.)

Scene Four

MARY'S HOTEL ROOM, THURSDAY MORNING. LAURIE SITS ON THE BED NEXT to Mary; they are wrapping favors in netting and tying them. Next to them on the table sits a bottle of wine and two glasses.

MARY: YOU SURE YOU'RE OKAY?

LAURIE: If you ask me that one more time I'm going to scream.

MARY: I'm just concerned.

LAURIE: Don't be. Look, my white count is up, my radiation is done, they think they've killed everything that they didn't already cut off. I'm as okay as a lopsided person can be . . . and to be perfectly honest I wish people wouldn't talk about it so much.

MARY: I wish I wasn't so far away.

LAURIE: Why you think I'm going to die on you?

MARY: Laurie!

LAURIE: What's wrong? It's the only thing we're guaranteed of in this lifetime you know. Death is the only thing we know for sure will come after birth—everything in between is gravy.

MARY: That's one way to look at it I guess.

LAURIE: Cancer doesn't have to mean death, Mary. I know that's what everyone thinks. But they're wrong.

MARY: Well, since you put it that way.

LAURIE: I'm thankful for my friends and all their love and support, but please, when I tell you it's okay believe me. *(Crosses to the table to curl the bows on the favors with a scissors.)* If anything I've learned to put my life in order. For instance, I used to teach this class in Russian literature . . . *Crime & Punishment* real uplifting stuff, and I hated it. So, I went to the administration, and I said, "I don't feel that I can do this class justice, I've never enjoyed it and I think my students have an equally miserable time, and I don't intend to teach it anymore. So, if you want to keep it in your curriculum, you're going to have to find another teacher."

MARY: And what did they say?

LAURIE: That's the thing. They said, "Fine."

MARY: Fine?

LAURIE: Evidently I have a strong following in the student body. They were quite upset when I was out. I got so many flowers and cards people in the hospital thought I was a celebrity. So, I guess the administration doesn't want to mess with me.

MARY: So you're learning how to manipulate people.

LAURIE: No, I'm learning how to prioritize. *(Crosses back to bed.)* Take your wedding, for example, I came because I love you and I wanted to be a part of your celebration. It was important for me to be here, and I would have come whether my radiation was done or not.

MARY: I'm glad you're here.

LAURIE: I am too. How many more of these do we have to make?

MARY: About twenty more. My in-laws wanted to buy everything, but I just couldn't be that detached from my own wedding.

LAURIE: It's a little bit like a fairy tale wedding. Beautiful, intelligent, doctor-to-be marries architect at the Chapel Royal at the Hampton Court Palace . . . There's got a be a Harlequin plot here somewhere.

MARY: Wait until you see the church it's gorgeous.

LAURIE: I'm sure it is.

MARY: So, are you seeing anyone?

LAURIE: No, Mary, my social calendar's been a bit full.

MARY: Just wondering. My brother's coming for the wedding.

LAURIE: Peter?

MARY: He's going to be one of the groom's men.

LAURIE: That's such a weird term. It's so stuffy.

MARY: He'll be here this afternoon, actually. I have to go Heathrow and get him.

LAURIE: It'll be nice to see him again.

MARY: I thought you might think so.

LAURIE: Hey, don't go getting any ideas.

MARY: I don't know what you mean.

LAURIE: Yes, you do. You think that because I've always thought Peter was attractive that I'm going to want to start dating him.

MARY: You're an adult now, Laurie; you can do what you want.

LAURIE: I'm only going to say this once, Mary. I am not interested in men at all right now.

MARY: Who are you kidding? You have always been interested in men. Unless, hey you and Meg haven't . . . you would tell me right?

LAURIE: Well, we were going to go pick out our pattern today at Harrods before announcing anything officially. . .

MARY: Very funny.

LAURIE: Meg and I are buddies. We've always been buddies. Oh, I know there was a time when everyone thought that maybe there would be more . . . but, I like men.

MARY: That's what I said.

LAURIE: And I like Meg too much to screw up our friendship. That's usually what happens when I fall for someone. I'm not ready for that yet. Understand?

MARY: Well, Peter has always had a thing for you.

LAURIE: Are you even listening to me?

MARY: Yeah. You don't want me to play matchmaker. I'm just telling you that my baby brother thinks you are terrific.

LAURIE: And, I'm warning you, back off.

(Lights fade.)

Scene Five

HEATHROW AIRPORT, WAITING ROOM, EARLY THURSDAY AFTERNOON. *Laurie stands waiting, holding a sign that says "Peter" and looking at her watch.*

Over the loud speaker we hear "May I have your attention please. British Airways flight 445 to Madrid is now boarding at Gate 21. British Airways flight 445 is now boarding at Gate 21."

Peter enters carrying a duffle bag and a guitar. HE recognizes her and smiles.

PETER: YOU'RE NOT MY SISTER.

LAURIE: No, she had to go for a last minute fitting. So, I was elected.

PETER: Well, I'm glad they picked you. Do you mind if we have sit for a moment? Flying always makes me a little shaky.

LAURIE: I know what you mean.

PETER: *(Sits down. Laurie sits next to him.)* I try to avoid it at all costs. But, when you have free room and board in a foreign country . . . I guess you bite the bullet.

LAURIE: *Dramamine* always seems to work for me. Knocks me right out.

PETER: I tried one of those patches. But, I still feel a little shaky.

LAURIE: So, you've been visiting before?

PETER: Couldn't let my only sister marry just anyone, could I?

LAURIE: I haven't met him yet, but Mary seems very happy.

PETER: That's all that matters to me. God, I haven't seen you since Mary's 21st birthday party.

LAURIE: That was quite an evening.

PETER: Leave it to Meg to throw a party. How is she?

LAURIE: She looks great.

PETER: Well, Meg always looks great. What I meant was . . . well, I went with Mary to Danielle's memorial service in November. I've never seen anyone so devastated. I didn't think she'd ever be the same.

LAURIE: Megan used to say that she'd found her other half, just like in that myth.

PETER: What myth?

LAURIE: It's not a myth, I think it's something Plato wrote . . . about two lovers being two halves of the same person.

PETER: I never heard that.

LAURIE: See the story says that all people were joined in pairs, but the neat part is that some were men and women, some were men and men, and some were women and women. And this race of people went to war with the gods, and the gods split them in two. So now these people roam the earth searching for their other half.

PETER: That would explain a lot of things, wouldn't it? So, anyway, tell me what's up with you. What have you been doing with yourself since you moved to Maryland?

LAURIE: Well, you know I'm a teacher.

PETER: I wish all my high school teachers were as pretty as you. I might have done better.

LAURIE: My understanding was that you did do rather well.

PETER: Mary always sings my praises a bit too loudly.

LAURIE: Juilliard's an impressive school.

PETER: More impressive if you actually graduate.

LAURIE: Oh, I thought . . .

PETER: It's not that I couldn't cut it or anything. I just started getting these studio gigs playing on people's albums. I got to play, have a blast and get paid. And my stuff is on discs now. But, I've been thinking about finishing.

LAURIE: Who have you played with?

PETER: Hey, now we're talking about me again. I want to hear about you. What do you teach?

LAURIE: English.

PETER: Really? I've always been a bit of an English buff myself. So, if I were to say, for instance—Poets for two-hundred. "To be alone with you at the close of day with only you in view while evening slips away. It only goes to show that while life's pleasures be few, the only one I know is when I'm alone with you."

LAURIE: That's pretty.

PETER: It's one of my favorites.

LAURIE: But, I think you might be stretching the realm of poetry, Peter.

PETER: What makes you say that?

LAURIE: Bob Dylan was a lyricist.

PETER: Well, then I'll have to try a real poet for three hundred. "Sing, for Faith and Hope are high, none so true as you and I. Sing the Lovers' Litany: 'Love like ours can never die!'"

LAURIE: Rudyard Kipling. And by my calculations you owe me five hundred dollars.

PETER: A math wizard, too! Would you settle for two tickets to *Sunset Boulevard*?

LAURIE: I was just kidding.

PETER: I wasn't. I know one of the musicians in the pit; I can get us decent seats. We could go to dinner and then hit the theatre afterwards.

LAURIE: I have your sister's bachelorette party.

PETER: After the wedding then?

LAURIE: I don't think that's a very good idea.

PETER: Did I say something to offend you?

LAURIE: No.

PETER: It was the quotes wasn't it? You don't like showing off.

LAURIE: No, it's just not a good time, okay.

PETER: Okay.

LAURIE: *(pauses)* We should be going.

PETER: But, as a man of honor, you must allow me to make good on my debt. Maybe a trip to the National Gallery, the Parliament . . . be adventurous and think of something. I'll be here for several days after the wedding.

LAURIE: So, will I.

(She exits.)

PETER: I know, Mary told me.

(Lights fade.)

Scene Six

THE GARDEN OF MARY'S FIANCÉ'S PARENT'S HOUSE. THURSDAY EVENING. Megan, dressed in a silky pantsuit, is seated on a bench starring at her drink. Gail, dressed in a black party dress, is standing near her.

MEGAN: WHY ARE YOU STILL PISSED OFF ABOUT STUART? IT WAS five years ago.

GAIL: Because, I haven't met anyone that could make me forget him. But, I suppose that it's more of the principle. Laurie was so pretty and charming in school she could have had anyone. So, why'd she have to take my man?

MEGAN: She didn't take him. You dumped him.

GAIL: You're a fine one to talk. Besides you always take Laurie's side. If you and Dannie didn't fall in love, I would have sworn that you would pine away for Laurie until the end of time.

MEGAN: *(takes a sip of her drink)* I was in love with her, I'll admit it.

GAIL: So why didn't you try harder. Maybe you could have gotten her, and I could have kept Stu.

MEGAN: Because, I met Danielle ... besides, Laurie doesn't love me that way.

GAIL: Well, I still wish you would have tried.

MEGAN: Can I ask you something?

GAIL: Could I stop you?

MEGAN: Can't you let it go? For Mary's sake. I mean we are here to celebrate with her. It's her time.

GAIL: You make it sound so easy.

MEGAN: I don't pretend that anything is easy. I'm just wondering if this was going to be so tough for you, why'd you come?

GAIL: Because, you people may not realize it but I miss you. I have hoards of friends in New York and we go out to all the "in" places, but I can't be myself around them. I mean, you guys know I can be a shit, but you still always include me . . .

PETER: *(enters)* Pardon me, ladies, but Mary has asked me to inform you that the dancing is about to begin.

MEGAN: Thank you.

PETER: I believe that she would like the both of you to come back inside.

GAIL: Come on, Meg.

MEGAN: You go. I'm gonna' stay out here for a couple of minutes.

GAIL: *(playfully scolds)* You don't want to disappoint your host.

MEGAN: I don't dance anymore.

GAIL: Okay, but you don't know what you're missing.

(Gail exits and Peter walks toward Megan.)

PETER: Are you okay, Megan?

MEGAN: I'm fine.

PETER: Can I ask you something?

MEGAN: Sure. *(Motions for him to sit down and he does.)*

PETER: I asked Laurie to go to dinner and the theatre with me after the wedding, and she shot me down pretty quickly. Do you have any suggestions?

MEGAN: Laurie's been through some rough times, what with Stu leaving her and all. Maybe you should just leave well enough alone.

PETER: She doesn't like me, does she?

MEGAN: Did I say that? I said, she's vulnerable now. Now might not be the best time.

PETER: When Mary told me that Laurie was going to be here, I changed my plane reservations to arrive a day earlier and leave a couple days later.

MEGAN: Hey, Pete, it's not like you and Laurie ever had a thing...

PETER: So, I'm a dreamer. Sue me.

MEGAN: Pete, my man, you have so much to learn about women. We're not possessions.

PETER: I never said you were.

MEGAN: You can't think that just because you want Laurie to notice you, she will. You have to win her affection.

PETER: How?

MEGAN: Do I look like Dear Abby?

PETER: Not quite. Do you believe in love at first sight?

MEGAN: I subscribe to it.

PETER: That's how I feel about Laurie. The first time Mary brought you guys to the lake house, I took one look at Laurie and I fell in love.

MEGAN: Why? Because she's attractive?

PETER: I'd be lying if I said she wasn't, but I know it's not just that. I mean, I like being around her. I felt like that story that she told me the other day, the one that you tell.

MEGAN: What story?

PETER: The thing that Plato said about the people that are connected.

MEGAN: You do have it bad.

PETER: That's what I'm trying to tell you.

MEGAN: I'm not telling you to pursue her. But, think about what you know about her and about what you think she might like . . . and give it a second shot, if you want.

PETER: Maybe I'll go ask her to dance.

MEGAN: That sounds like a start.

PETER: You coming?

MEGAN: No, I'm fine here.

*(Peter exits. Megan moves about the garden. Laurie
enters and places her hands on Megan's shoulders.)*

LAURIE: Penny for your thoughts.

MEGAN: *(looks at Laurie)* I fear you wouldn't be getting your monies worth. Did you see Peter?

LAURIE: No.

MEGAN: You must have just passed each other.

LAURIE: Don't try and be a Yenta, it doesn't suit you.

MEGAN: All I said was he was looking for you.

LAURIE: Okay. You have to be thinking about something. You've been out here the better part of the night.

MEGAN: *(Crosses away from Laurie).* I don't want to talk about it.

LAURIE: *(Follows Megan)* Meg, if you're upset about me. Don't be.

MEGAN: I told you before, you may think God's mad at you, but she's not that mad at me. *(Squeezes Laurie's hand)* I know you're going to be all right.

LAURIE: I hope so.

> *(Megan keeps Laurie's hand in hers and sits on the bench. Laurie sits next to her.)*

MEGAN: So that Peter's kind of cute, huh?

LAURIE: Can you guys cut me a break?

MEGAN: I just said he was cute.

LAURIE: What do you know? He didn't come on to you.

MEGAN: So he made a pass at you, if you could call it that. The way you were talking before you'd think he'd killed your mother or something.

LAURIE: I am not ready for this right now.

MEGAN: Why not?

LAURIE: Because I don't feel attractive.

MEGAN: That's ridiculous, you look great.

LAURIE: You haven't seen me naked.

MEGAN: So take off your clothes, let me be the judge.

LAURIE: Right here? Besides, you already know what this kind of scar looks like. So, you wouldn't be shocked.

MEGAN: Is your scar that ugly?

LAURIE: I think it is. I feel disfigured.

MEGAN: *(Stands)* I can't believe that you're buying into all this crap about your breasts making you a woman.

LAURIE: Easy for you to say, you're gay.

MEGAN: And you're an English teacher. So what?

LAURIE: You know what I mean.

MEGAN: Look, I happen to know Peter. I spent many a holiday with the Lewis family and Peter's a great guy. He's soft spoken, an artist, sensitive, not to mention pretty damn good looking. Not at all like that asshole Stu . . . what do you want an engraved invitation?

LAURIE: And when he wants to take me to bed what am I supposed to say? By the way I sacrificed my left breast to the great god of cancer in exchange for my life.

MEGAN: You're so dramatic. I didn't say to fuck him; I said it can't hurt to get to know him. You do remember the art of conversation?

LAURIE: Just change the subject, okay?

MEGAN: *(sits down on the bench beside Laurie).* No. I want to know what that pompous ass did to you?

LAURIE: It's what he didn't do, okay?

MEGAN: You mean after the operation, he never . . .

LAURIE: Made love to me. He couldn't look at me, even with clothes on; it was like he was looking right through me.

MEGAN: God help that son-of-a-bitch if I ever find him.

LAURIE: Don't waste your time on him.

MEGAN: Laurie, you can't go by him. *(Touches Laurie's hair)* You are still an incredibly beautiful woman. Any man would be lucky to have you.

LAURIE: *(Crosses away from Megan).* I was so tough when it all happened. I asked all the right questions, I read everything I could get my hands on, I was determined that this would not get the best of me. I'm still determined. But when I go out to the mall and I look around at other women in beautiful dresses and swimsuits . . . and what about when I do want to make love with someone again? When do I tell them, what do I tell them?

MEGAN: *(crosses towards Laurie).* Look, Stu was a fluke. There are a lot of nice guys out there. Peter seems like one of them. Lord knows he's always had a thing for you. *(Touches the back of Laurie's shoulder).* But whether it's Peter or Larry, Moe or Curly you're going to have to put yourself out there again. You're going to have to take a chance.

LAURIE: *(pulls away from Megan, and turns to face her.)* I don't know what to tell people. Can't you understand that?

MEGAN: Well, I know, and I'd be honored to be with you.

LAURIE: Shut up, Meg.

MEGAN: You think I'm teasing you, don't you?

LAURIE: That's what we do, Meg. We tease each other.

MEGAN: We don't have to. I've always loved you know that.

LAURIE: I love you too. You're my best friend.

MEGAN: And it kills me to see you hurting like this.

LAURIE: I can't help how I feel.

MEGAN: *(grabs Laurie's shoulders)* There's no reason to feel that way.

LAURIE: How can I make you see what I mean?

MEGAN: I only see what's in front of me. A beautiful, intelligent, loving woman . . .

> *(Kisses Laurie. When Laurie pulls away she looks at her*
> *for a moment, then runs out. Megan smacks herself*
> *in the head.)*

Stupid, Megan, really stupid...

> *(Lights fade.)*

Scene Seven

Laurie and Megan's hotel room later Thursday evening. Laurie is sitting on the bed, dressed in a robe, ready for bed. She is reading and she checks her watch. Megan enters.

LAURIE: Where have you been?

MEGAN: Walking. *(Begins to pack her things.)*

LAURIE: I was worried about you, when you didn't come back with the others.

MEGAN: Oh.

LAURIE: Meg, you kissed me.

MEGAN: And you ran away.

LAURIE: That was stupid of me, but, why did you do it?

MEGAN: 'Cuz I wasn't thinking.

LAURIE: What are you doing?

MEGAN: The front desk said there's another room on the third floor.

LAURIE: You're changing rooms?

MEGAN: I thought you'd be more comfortable.

LAURIE: Why are you going to try and jump me in my sleep?

MEGAN: Forgive me if I don't want to banter.

(Tries to exit. Laurie cuts her off.)

LAURIE: Meg, stop being an idiot and talk to me.

MEGAN: What?

LAURIE: I'm a little confused. I thought you were upset about Dannie.

MEGAN: I was.

LAURIE: So why kiss me?

MEGAN: Because you're attractive . . . desirable . . . scared . . . and I'm hurting.

LAURIE: I told you in school that I . . .

MEGAN: don't love me that way. I heard you.

LAURIE: Then why?

MEGAN: Because I'm a fucking idiot, okay? *(Moves away from Laurie, sets the suitcase down.)*

LAURIE: I'm just trying to understand.

MEGAN: Look, I crossed that invisible line that we set up years ago. And I probably blew the best relationship I have left in my life, but Jesus Laurie, I can't take it back. I'm sorry. I just don't know how to make you see that you're still you. You're still beautiful and sexy . . . and you're the best friend I have in the world. I just pray I haven't screwed things up too badly.

LAURIE: You didn't screw things up.

MEGAN: Yes, I did. I'm just so crazy about you, Laurie. I can't stand to see you hurting like this.

LAURIE: So you thought kissing me would help?

MEGAN: You think that no one knows how you feel. Well, you're wrong. I was scared when Dannie came back from the hospital. I mean I thought of her body like a work of art chiseled by Michelangelo. I used to spend hours just watching her. She was just as scared as you are . . . but I was so thankful that she was alive. I know that she had scars . . . but I don't remember them being anything more than a new part of her. And I just felt so blessed to be able to hold her in my arms again . . . that meant more than anything. Don't you see, I just wanted to make you feel loved . . . and I guess I wanted . . . *(she crosses towards Laurie, but stops herself from reaching out.)*

LAURIE: You really miss her, don't you?

MEGAN: More than anything.

LAURIE: I was relieved when you met Danielle.

MEGAN: Why?

LAURIE: Partly because I was off the hook . . .

MEGAN: Off the hook?

LAURIE: Yeah. I knew how you felt about me long before you told me. I wish I could feel the same way.

MEGAN: That makes two of us.

LAURIE: My friendship's always been enough for you.

MEGAN: *(Sits down on the bed.)* It still is. I guess I was missing Dannie and you were hurting, tell me the other reason you were glad I met Dannie.

LAURIE: *(Sits in the chair next to the bed.)* Because she understood you. And, she brought out the best in you.

MEGAN: I know. I'm afraid that I've lost that now.

LAURIE: You can't lose something that was always there to begin with.

MEGAN: I just feel lost without her.

LAURIE: I knew you would.

MEGAN: And Mother keeps sending me on these assignments to photograph this star or that upcoming talent. I'm beginning to feel like I work for *People* magazine. Not an award-winning magazine like *Millennium*.

LAURIE: She's just concerned, Meg. She's always been that way.

MEGAN: I close my eyes at night and I try to picture Dannie like she was the first day I photographed her . . . so young and full of promise. But all I can see is her wasting away. And, I'm not sad so much as angry. Angry that she's gone. Angry that I'll never know what it's like to grow old together . . . that I'll never know that kind of love again ... I'm angry that I had to hold her hand while they pumped that stuff into her system . . . that I had to convince her that I still loved her ... that I had to watch her die, damn-it! She was only thirty-one. But, I'm not angry with God anymore. Now, I'm angry with the doctors . . . angry they don't know more. That they couldn't save her. That we live in a country that cares more about weapons than about it's people . . . they can spend billions of dollars on a plane that can destroy lives . . . but they can't find a cure for a disease that's killing people ... we didn't even know there was such a thing as inflammatory cancer . . . *(moves away from Laurie)* I'm sorry. I don't think we should have this conversation.

LAURIE: Why not? You don't think I feel the anger? No one knows that much about it. I read all the literature.

MEGAN: Who knew there were different kinds? Maybe if we knew we'd have something to look for.

LAURIE: We're too young to have to worry about breast cancer. You're not even supposed to get a mammogram until your forty!

MEGAN: No matter who gets it, it still sucks.

LAURIE: I'm not saying that anyone should get it. Jesus, do you think I wanted it? *(Megan doesn't answer.)* Well, do you, Meg? Meg, look at me.

(Megan moves further away. Laurie moves toward her.)

Look at me, damnit!

(Laurie forces Megan to turn around. Megan is crying.)

MEGAN: I can't. I keep thinking that I'm going to lose you, too.

LAURIE: *(pulls MEGAN into her arms)* That's silly. I'm gonna' be okay.

MEGAN: *(pulls away)* Don't comfort me. You're the one that I should be comforting.

LAURIE: We both know how that turned out. Besides, you don't have to be tough for me. I can't even imagine what you've been through. I mean I think about Stuart leaving me, and I can't even compare it. You lost your true love.

MEGAN: I told myself I wasn't going to do this.

LAURIE: It's okay, Meg. *(Touches her shoulder)* Hey, it's okay. Best friends are hard to come by; you are not going to lose me. I'm fighting this thing, and I'm gonna' beat it. All I want is a normal life. I need you to believe that I can have it. I need you to believe in me.

MEGAN: I want to. Oh God, Laurie, I want to. Dannie thought she was going to beat it too, until the second operation and the fourth round of chemo . . .

LAURIE: She didn't want to leave you, Meg.

MEGAN: Then why isn't she here?

LAURIE: *(hugs Megan)* Oh, Meg, she loved you. Sometimes, you just can't fight it. Maybe if they would have found it sooner . . . I know if they would have found it sooner, she would still be here. She was a fighter.

MEGAN: I miss her so much.

LAURIE: *(rocks Megan gently)* I know. I know. It's okay. Just let it all out.

(Lights fade.)

Scene Eight

A PARK BENCH, FRIDAY MORNING. MEGAN IS PHOTOGRAPHING LAURIE AND Mary. They are clowning around, as she snaps photos.

MARY: SHE'S JUST A SHIT AT TIMES.

LAURIE: You invited her.

MARY: Yeah, well, I thought that she'd matured.

MEGAN: Haven't you kept in touch with her?

MARY: Not like I keep in touch with you guys.

LAURIE: Why'd you ask her?

MARY: Because she asked me, remember?

MEGAN: Yeah, Laurie, don't you remember her ten-minute marriage to that drug dealer.

MARY: Rick wasn't a drug dealer.

MEGAN: Oh, no he just had a bad sinus condition.

(Peter enters.)

PETER: Good morning, Sis. *(Kisses Mary)* And ladies. *(Hands Mary a set of keys)* Here are the keys for the car, thanks. You'll be pleased to know that the tux looks great.

MARY: Good now we can move on to the Tower of London.

MEGAN: Yes, wouldn't want to miss those crown jewels.

LAURIE: Maybe I should skip the tower.

PETER: I was going to see the Royal Shakespeare Company. I'd love it if you came with me.

LAURIE: That's sweet, Peter, but...

PETER: *As You Like It.*

LAURIE: Well, I...

PETER: I understand, you not a fan of the Bards, right?

MEGAN: Laurie loves Shakespeare. She just doesn't want to hurt your sister's feelings, do you, Laurie?

MARY: You wouldn't hurt my feelings. Pete, could you be a doll and run across the street and get me some more film?

PETER: Sure.

(Peter exits.)

LAURIE: No lectures.

MEGAN: Okay, Laurie do you want to go with us to see the jewels and your buddy Gail? Or . . .

LAURIE: Not really.

MARY: Maybe you should just tell Gail.

LAURIE: What?

MARY: About you.

LAURIE: No way. For what? So she can feel sorry for me?

MEGAN: How do you know she'll feel sorry for you?

LAURIE: I'm warning both of you. I don't want her to know.

MEGAN: Well, Doc, I guess we've been told.

MARY: I guess so.

MEGAN: So, then you want to go with Peter?

LAURIE: I don't want to do that either.

MARY: What's wrong with my brother?

LAURIE: There's nothing wrong with your brother. He's terrific, okay?

MARY: Look, why don't you just go with him. It's just a play, and you love Shakespeare.

PETER: *(enters with the film, which he hands to Mary)* Here you go.

MARY: Thanks.

LAURIE: Peter, I'd like to go with you.

PETER: Really?

LAURIE: I'm a big Shakespeare fan, and I've wanted to see The Royal Shakespeare Company.

PETER: Great.

MARY: Well, Meg and I should run then. So that Gail doesn't feel like we've all abandoned her. Have fun.

MEGAN: Meet you back at the hotel later.

(Megan and Mary exit.)

PETER: You get the feeling they're rooting for us?

LAURIE: That's putting it mildly.

PETER: Look, if you're uncomfortable, I could give you the tickets, and I could do something else.

LAURIE: They're your tickets.

PETER: I know. I just don't know why I make you so uncomfortable.

LAURIE: It's not you, Peter.

PETER: So then it's all men?

LAURIE: No. Only the ones . . .

PETER: Only which ones?

LAURIE: We should get going.

PETER: But, I want to know.

LAURIE: It's not important. Let's see if we can go make the guards at the palace crack up before we go the play.

PETER: I don't know we tried that last time I was here. Those guys don't laugh at anything.

LAURIE: Well, we could try.

PETER: I'm game if you are.

LAURIE: Great.

(He exits. She follows as lights fade.)

Scene Nine

Planet Hollywood, Friday evening. Gail, Megan, and Mary have been dancing. They enter from the dance floor, drinks in hand, and cross to a table.

GAIL: I bet the guys have a stripper; we should have gotten a stripper.

MARY: *(laughs)* I don't need a stripper.

GAIL: Too bad. Well, it's your last night of freedom, Mary, but if it were mine, I'd want a stripper.MARY:

I'm just happy all of my friends could be here. *(Raises her glass)* To friendship.

(All toast.)

GAIL: Well, I'm gonna' go find some stud to dance with. Since Laurie's in the ladies room maybe I'll have a chance.

MEGAN: Hey, we're here to have a good time, remember.

(Laurie enters.)

GAIL: *(to Laurie)* You even have women falling at your feet, now.

MEGAN: You can be a real pig sometime, Gail, you know that.

GAIL: Why, because I say what I think?

LAURIE: She's just being pissy to everyone, because she's mad at me.

GAIL: Damn right, I am.

MARY: I've asked you nicely to not do this. Now, sit down, Gail.

GAIL: *(mimics Mary)* Sit down, Gail. Everyone always takes Laurie's side. I don't even know why you asked me here.

MARY: Because I thought we were friends.

GAIL: Well, if we're such good friends why don't we stay in touch? Why don't we see each other more often? Why don't I know more about your lives?

LAURIE: What you really want to know is why Stuart left me. So why don't you just ask, and leave the others out of it.

GAIL: Okay, why did Stuart leave you?

LAURIE: Well, if you must know. It's because I had a mastectomy and your prince charming turned out to be a real frog.

GAIL: Very funny. Don't fuck with me.

LAURIE: What's the matter, Gail? Truth too much for you?

GAIL: *(doesn't think it's true)* I can't believe you guys would joke. You're serious. I . . . You all knew this, and no one told me.

MEGAN: I just found out. Only Doc knew.

GAIL: *(to Laurie)* But you weren't gonna' tell me, where you?

LAURIE: What for?

GAIL: This is exactly what I mean. We don't know each other anymore. We've grown apart.

MARY: I'm sorry you feel that way, Gail. I always thought there wasn't anything that the four musketeers couldn't work through.

LAURIE: Wait a minute what's to work through? I have the cancer not you.

MARY: I know that, I just meant . . .

LAURIE: Meant what? You don't have this. I do. I'm the one that lost a breast. I'm the one that went through the radiation . . .

MEGAN: Laurie, don't jump down Mary's throat. Just calm down.

LAURIE: I am calm. I've been calm this whole time. I mean I came across the fucking ocean to celebrate Mary's wedding. That's what I want to do. I don't want to think about cancer, I don't want to talk about it. I don't want anyone to feel sorry for me. *(Crosses to Gail)*

GAIL: I don't feel sorry for you. I'm mad as hell that you wouldn't tell me. We told each other everything in college.

LAURIE: Like hell we did.

GAIL: Well we did until . . . *(stops herself)*

LAURIE: *(Gets in Gail's face)* Until what? I stole your boyfriend, is that what you were going to say?

GAIL: I didn't say that.

LAURIE: Jesus Christ, you're afraid to confront me. You've always been afraid to confront me. We didn't tell each other anything after Stuart started seeing me, all we did was walk on eggshells around each other. Well, I have news for you, Gail, if you want to call Stu, you have my blessing. Marry the son-of-a-bitch if you want. Just don't call me when he dumps you in your hour of need, okay?

(Starts to leave.)

GAIL: Laurie...

LAURIE: Save it.

(Laurie exits.)

MARY: I knew this was a bad idea to have you both here. But, I said to myself, no, Mary, don't be silly, they're both your friends, they're both adults now . . .

GAIL: Don't try and pin this on me. You knew and you didn't tell me. You could have told me.

MEGAN: And what was she supposed to say to you? Grow up, Gail, Laurie has breast cancer.

GAIL: Why is everything my fault?

MARY: Look, Laurie asked me not to say anything. I'm a doctor; I'm supposed to be trained to keep things confidential.

GAIL: So what do you want a fucking medal?

MARY: Don't you think I wanted to call someone and talk to them when she told me? I was frightened for her. But, I'm the doctor, I'm supposed to be rational, calm . . . I'm the one that's supposed to tell my best friend that she should listen to the doctors and cut off a part of her body.

MEGAN: Mary, you did the right thing.

MARY: Did I? I'm a pediatrician, not a breast surgeon. All I know is what I read in my medical journals.

MEGAN: You have nothing to feel bad about, Mary.

GAIL: Well, is she okay or what?

MEGAN: Always the compassionate one.

GAIL: Fuck you.

MEGAN: Not if you were the last woman on earth.

GAIL: *(to Megan)* I'm sorry. Isn't this the same thing that Dannie died from?

MEGAN: It's not the same kind.

GAIL: Well, can Laurie die from this?

MEGAN: Bite your tongue.

GAIL: Well, can she?

MARY: It can metastasize somewhere else if they haven't caught it all, but she caught it early, which is excellent.

GAIL: It can what-a-size?

MEGAN: It can grow somewhere else like on her lungs or chest wall if the radiation hasn't killed all the mutant cells. But, it looks pretty good for her. *(Rises)* Look, I'm gonna' go make sure she's okay.

GAIL: Meg, I'm really sorry about Dannie. I should have been there.

MEGAN: That would have been nice.

GAIL: I've been a real shit.

MEGAN: Hey, don't beat yourself up. This isn't anyone's fault. It just happens.

GAIL: After five years you'd think I'd stop being angry with Stuart.

MEGAN: Yeah, well, there's no accounting for taste.

MARY: Let me know if you need anything.

MEGAN: I will.

(Megan exits. Mary turns to Gail.)

MARY: You know, just because you've been a shit thus far in life, doesn't mean you always have to be one.

GAIL: Is that advice from my doctor?

MARY: No, that's advice from someone that doesn't want to see you go through life miserable. Just put this Stuart thing behind you, and move on.

(Lights fade.)

Scene Ten

LAURIE AND MEGAN'S HOTEL ROOM, LATER FRIDAY EVENING. MEGAN IS looking through the pictures on her digital camera and Laurie is writing in her journal.

MEGAN: WHAT DO YOU WRITE IN THAT THING ANYWAY?

LAURIE: Thoughts. Impressions of events. Nothing profound.

MEGAN: Are all English teachers frustrated writers?

LAURIE: I don't know about all.

> *(There is a knock at the door. Megan opens it. Gail is standing there.)*

GAIL: May I come in?

MEGAN: *(looks to Laurie who nods yes)* Sure.

GAIL: Look, I know it's late, but . . . *(To Megan)* Do you think I could have some time alone with Laurie?

MEGAN: *(picks up her jacket and her camera case.)* I'll just take a walk. Try not to break anything, okay?

(Megan exits.)

GAIL: Look, Laurie, I ah...

LAURIE: If you're here to apologize because you think I'm about to die or something, you can leave.

GAIL: That's not why I'm here. May I? *(Sits down)* I came to find out why we never got past this?

LAURIE: Maybe it made things easier. I took Stuart, you felt hurt, and I felt guilty.

GAIL: So why didn't we fight about it then and get it out of our systems?

LAURIE: I never thought I was any good at fighting. Boy, was I wrong.

GAIL: And I was the Queen, except when it came to you.

LAURIE: I don't understand why you were so hurt. You kicked him out.

GAIL: And you thought I meant it?

LAURIE: The guy shows up on my doorstep for the umpteenth time and wants comfort. What was I supposed to do?

GAIL: Turn him away.

LAURIE: You think I didn't try.

GAIL: Well, he stayed with you.

LAURIE: Maybe because I didn't mess with his head all the time.

GAIL: And I did?

LAURIE: Are you for real? You yanked him around like he was a fucking yo-yo.

GAIL: And you kept him on a leash.

LAURIE: You don't know what you're talking about.

GAIL: Why didn't he ever talk to me then? Huh?

LAURIE: Maybe he didn't want to.

GAIL: You didn't let him, and you know it.

LAURIE: You're crazy, you know that.

GAIL: I'm crazy! He was the only guy I ever cared about.

LAURIE: What about Rick?

GAIL: You see how that turned out?

LAURIE: Maybe that should tell you something.

GAIL: What the hell is that supposed to mean?

LAURIE: That means that, that saying, if you love something set it free and it will come back to you. It doesn't apply when you keep kicking that something out.

GAIL: Are you saying I deserved it?

LAURIE: I'm saying that you got what was coming to you. Yeah.

GAIL: You bitch.

LAURIE: He loved you, stupid. You just fucked with his head once to often. I never meant for anything to happen between us. The way you've described it all these years—I was the great seducer. Well, I have news for you, Gail; people aren't seduced unless they want to be.

GAIL: So what are you trying to tell me?

LAURIE: That Stuart wouldn't have come back to you.

GAIL: You don't know that.

LAURIE: Yes, I do. He told me. That was the last time for him. If it wasn't me, it would have been someone else.

GAIL: That might have been easier to take.

LAURIE: I have news for you—wish it was someone else. I wish that he had never come between us. I lost a great friend because of him.

GAIL: You mean that?

LAURIE: Yeah. Oh, I thought he was worth it then, but he's certainly not the man to have around in a crisis.

GAIL: He really left you because of that?

LAURIE: *(Rises)* I don't know. Maybe we had our problems before that. I mean who lives with someone that long and doesn't talk about marriage, or at least children. I was ready two years ago to start a family, but I guess Stuart wasn't. He was always so driven by his career. I suppose having to stop and deal with something in his personal life was too much for him to handle.

GAIL: Don't apologize for him.

LAURIE: *(sits in the chair near the bed)* I don't. I think what he did was wrong. I wish I had someone to stand by me no matter what. I went through radiation with women that had that kind of support from their husbands. A couple of times I went to this support group at the hospital, but all the women were in their 50's and 60's, a couple in their 40's. They all had husbands . . . I just didn't feel like I could relate. All of them hated Stuart immediately when I told them.

GAIL: Can you blame them? I wouldn't touch him now with a ten-foot pole. Look, Laurie, I'd like to put this Stuart thing behind us if it's possible.

LAURIE: I'd like that too.

GAIL: *(holds out her hand)* Hi, I'm Gail Williams.

LAURIE: *(shakes Gail's hand)* Laurie Kovak.

GAIL: Pleased to meet you. Would it be okay to hug you?

LAURIE: *(stands up to hug Gail)* Just watch the fake boob, sometimes it jabs people.

GAIL: *(hesitates)* Really?

LAURIE: No, I'm just teasing you, goof-ball.

GAIL: *(relieved)* Oh.

> *(They hug. Laurie pulls away and sits down on the bed. Gail sits next to her.)*

LAURIE: So, what now?

GAIL: Well, don't get upset, but, we were talking about your cancer when you left.

LAURIE: What else is new. Did you come up with any new solutions?

GAIL: We're your friends, Laurie, we're just concerned, and we're here for you.

LAURIE: I know.

GAIL: I would have never known if you didn't say something. Did you have reconstructive surgery?

LAURIE: They said that they could have done it right away. But, I didn't want implants, and I'm just not sure about the other methods since they're so new. I never was in the hospital before this, so I wanted to see how I did and down the road maybe . . .

GAIL: What does it look like?

LAURIE: Excuse me?

GAIL: Your scar.

LAURIE: You want to know what my scar looks like?

GAIL: I'm afraid. First Dannie and now you . . . not that I think you're gonna' die or anything . . .

LAURIE: You want to see what made Stuart run. Don't you?

GAIL: Yeah.

LAURIE: *(Stands and moves away from her)* Is it really that important to you?

GAIL: Hey, it's not like I'm Meg or anything. I just want to see.

LAURIE: Okay. *(Loosens the belt on her robe)* But, you better be sure.

GAIL: I'm sure.

> *(Laurie opens her robe, so that Gail can see. Gail's*
> *mouth drops open, and Laurie quickly closes her*
> *robe again.)*

LAURIE: Happy now?

GAIL: No I'm not happy, I'm sorry.

LAURIE: So am I.

> *(A silence falls between them.)*

It's getting late. Maybe we can catch up tomorrow.

GAIL: Okay. I guess you need your rest.

LAURIE: Sometimes I just feel exhausted.

GAIL: Okay. *(Takes LAURIE's hand)* Sleep tight.

> *(Lights fade.)*

Scene Eleven

THE GARDEN OF MARY'S FIANCÉ'S PARENTS, SATURDAY EVENING. IT'S Mary's wedding reception. Laurie, dressed in her bridesmaid dress sits on the bench.

A jazz quartet is heard playing off stage.

Megan enters dragging Peter behind her. He is dressed in a tuxedo, and looks tentative.

MEGAN: LAURIE, PETER NEEDS A DANCE PARTNER, AND YOU KNOW I don't dance.

LAURIE: You do so.

MEGAN: I told you, I don't dance since Dannie.

PETER: *(starts to leave)* I told her this wasn't a good idea.

MEGAN: *(grabs his hand)* Yes it is. *(Turns to Laurie and whispers)* One dance. How can it possibly hurt?

LAURIE: *(whispers back)* One dance and you'll get out of my hair.

MEGAN: I'll never bother you about this particular subject again.

LAURIE: Fine, but if I dance with Peter, you have to dance with me.

MEGAN: You're crazy.

LAURIE: That's the deal.

MEGAN: You drive a hard bargain. But, I'll dance with you.

LAURIE: *(squeezes Megan's hand, then stands and says to Peter)* Well, Peter, looks like my dance card is free after all.

(Megan exits.)

PETER: *(obviously hurt)* Look, Laurie, obviously you don't like me for some reason. Let's just pretend we danced and I'll tell Meg you did, okay?

(Peter tries to exit.)

LAURIE: It's not that I don't like you, Peter.

PETER: Really?

LAURIE: We can dance.

(Peter crosses back and offers Laurie his hand. They begin to dance.)

What exactly did Meg tell you?

PETER: She tried to tell me that you were shy, and that secretly deep down you liked me.

LAURIE: She said that, huh?

PETER: Yeah, she can really shovel it.

LAURIE: She didn't say anything else?

PETER: No. *(They dance in silence for some time, then Peter pulls her closer)* Is this okay?

(Laurie nods.)

Listen about the other day. I wasn't trying to test you or anything. I was just playing. I do that a lot. I guess I just haven't learned when to stop.

LAURIE: I had a nice time.

PETER: Then why'd you turn me down? Tickets to *Sunset Boulevard* aren't easy to come by you know?

LAURIE: I'm sure they're not.

PETER: Jesus, Laurie, you have to know I'm crazy about you. When Mary told me you broke up with Stu, well, I just thought that maybe you and . . .

LAURIE: *(moves away from Peter)* Peter, we hardly know each other.

PETER: I know all about you from Mary, and the summers you spent with us. Maybe if you give me a chance, you might find out I'm an okay guy.

LAURIE: You don't know anything about me, Peter. You might not like me once you get to know me.

PETER: I doubt that.

LAURIE: What if you found out that I wasn't what I appeared to be?

PETER: Megan told me that you were a woman of many surprises.

LAURIE: But did she say they were all pleasant?

PETER: She said, that no matter what they were, you were worth it.

LAURIE: She said that?

PETER: And I would have to agree.

*(He extends his hand, after a moment she takes it. They
dance in silence for a moment.)*

LAURIE: So did Meg say anything else?

PETER: Only that if I hurt you she'd hunt me down like the low down, dirty, dog …

LAURIE: In that case, I'd better leave while your reputation is intact.

(Laurie breaks contact.)

PETER: Why don't you just tell me your deep, dark secret?

LAURIE: *(turns to look at him)* Who said I have a deep dark secret?

PETER: Well, you think that something is going to frighten me off. Why don't you tell me what it is? Do you remember when Mary brought you up to the lake house? Not the first time, but your junior year?

LAURIE: And you and I got stranded in the old pick-up truck going to town for supplies.

PETER: Do you remember what you said to me?

LAURIE: No.

PETER: *(clutches his heart)* I'm crushed.

LAURIE: *(Crosses back to him).* What did I say?

PETER: You looked at me with those incredible eyes, and you said, "Pete, the girl that marries you is going to be one of the luckiest girls on earth."

LAURIE: I remember now.

PETER: I know that you think something terrible is going to frighten me off. So why not find out if you're right.

LAURIE: *(moves away from him)* I don't think this is a good idea.

PETER: I do. I'll even help. Let's see ... you're an axe murderer?

LAURIE: No.

PETER: A drug dealer?

LAURIE: No. Don't do this.

PETER: I know, you're actually glad that bell-bottoms are back.

LAURIE: *(Turns and blurts out).* I had breast cancer, and I'm one boob short of a set.

(Peter doesn't know what to say, he is clearly stunned.)

Not so glib now, are you?

PETER: I ... I...

LAURIE: Oh, just go ahead, get out of here.

PETER: What?

LAURIE: You know you want to go.

(Peter shakes his head to say no.)

I don't want your pity.

PETER: Look, I . . . uh . . .

LAURIE: What? Don't know what to say? Just leave me alone!

PETER: That's what you want, isn't it?

LAURIE: No, it's just inevitable.

PETER: Why?

LAURIE: Do you want me to spell it out for you?

PETER: Uh-huh.

LAURIE: (starts to leave) I don't have time for this.

PETER: You took me by surprise. I thought you were going to tell me that you were hung up about our ages. I was already to tell you I didn't care about that.

LAURIE: But you can't say that about this, can you?

PETER: I can't believe that you think I'm that shallow?

LAURIE: No, I think you're only human.

PETER: I don't understand you, Laurie. You had a disease that required a drastic treatment, but you chose survival and you appear to be doing very well. Are you going to go through life afraid of men now?

LAURIE: Look, Peter, you don't have to prove anything to me. You're the one that forced the issue.

PETER: What issue?

LAURIE: I can't do this, Peter. (She tries to exit, but he blocks her)

PETER: Who you gonna' do it with?

LAURIE: What?

PETER: Is it going to be easier to tell a total stranger?

LAURIE: Maybe. I don't know.

PETER: I love you. I don't care if you have one breast or two or none at all. I'm not in love with your breasts! And, I'm sorry if I didn't know what to say right away . . .

LAURIE: You can't honestly tell me that you want damaged goods.

PETER: I didn't realize I was purchasing anything.

LAURIE: You know what I mean.

PETER: Yeah, you think I'm going to take one look at you naked and run for the hills. So, you'd like to avoid that scene and make me run ahead of time. Well, surprise! I'm not a runner.

LAURIE: You say that now.

PETER: Jesus Christ, Laurie, I changed my plans just to have some extra time here in hopes that you would spend it with me. You and Megan are the only two women that I don't feel like a total tongue-tied idiot around...

LAURIE: Maybe there's time for you to pick up Megan.

PETER: I'm gonna' pretend that you didn't make such an asinine suggestion. Now, sit down and listen to me. *(He motions for her to sit down, and sits beside her)* I have always been attracted to you, not just because I find you attractive, but also because I have always been comfortable around you, you make me laugh, you make think about life. I know what you had done must have been terrible for you and your self-image, but why would I think any less of you for wanting to live?

(Laurie is speechless.)

If I was speechless or shocked, it's because you said the "C" word. And, maybe because I thought this was something only older women got . . .

LAURIE: You don't hear about younger women, because they usually don't find it in time.

PETER: But you did, right?

LAURIE: I'm not planning on dying, if that's what you're asking.

PETER: I don't think anyone really does. But you are all right, aren't you?

LAURIE: What if I'm not?

PETER: *(moves his chair closer, and takes her hand.)* Laurie, I want you to be able to talk to me. I want to be your friend.

LAURIE: *(moves away from him)* Oh, now, you just want to be my friend . . .

PETER: No. When you're ready ... I'd like to be more than that.

LAURIE: What if I'm never ready?

PETER: I'll take that chance.

LAURIE: Why?

PETER: Because, I think you are my other half...

LAURIE: That's Megan's story not mine. *(She sits on the bench)*

PETER: You're not very romantic for an English teacher.

LAURIE: You don't know what you're talking about.

PETER: *(Moves toward her)* I'm talking about amore, affairs of the heart, love . . . I'm crazy about you, Laurie. I always have been. May I kiss you? *(Sits on the bench beside her)*

LAURIE: Well, now I know that you're crazy.

PETER: You really know how to pour on the charm.

LAURIE: I want to believe you, Peter...

PETER: Then do.

LAURIE: Stuart thought he loved me too, until . . .

PETER: Any man that would walk away from you is a total idiot in my book, and I don't want to hear his name used again in a comparative sentence with mine. Understand?

LAURIE: I don't know about this.

PETER: I can move as fast, or as slow as you want, Laurie. You just tell me what you need.

LAURIE: You can start by pinching me, because this is getting to be a little too much for me to believe.

PETER: I'll go you one better than that. *(kisses her)* Is that real enough for you?

LAURIE: That's pretty real.

PETER: So, about those tickets for *Sunset Boulevard* . . .

LAURIE: I guess it couldn't hurt to go. Okay.

PETER: Good. Let's dance some more.

LAURIE: *(takes his hand)* I'd like that.

PETER: *(pulls her close, and They begin to dance)* See, I'm not that bad once you get to know me.

LAURIE: I'm counting on it.

Curtain.

A Note on the Casting

<small>I HAVE INCLUDED SOME CHARACTER NOTES TO HELP GUIDE YOU:</small>

The actress playing Laurie should be cast with the knowledge that she will have to appear to only have one breast for several scenes in the play. She is in every scene of the play, so serious consideration as to how you will achieve this effect, should be well thought out.

Megan should never be played in a stereotypical manner based on her sexuality. She is neither overly masculine or feminine.

There needs to be an obvious chemistry between the characters of Laurie and Megan, as well as between Laurie and Megan.

A Note on Publicity

THE PLAY WORKS WELL WHEN PERFORMED IN OCTOBER IN CONJUNCTION with National Breast Cancer Awareness Month. This offers a chance to tie-in to the community with support group talk-backs held with local survivors and the cast. The talk-back idea works no matter when you decide to present it, however it helps with publicity to utilize this month.

Some productions have offered a portion of the proceeds to a breast cancer organization of their choice, which has helped to increase ticket sales.

About the Playwright

NOVELIST AND PLAYWRIGHT, EA KAFKALAS IS THE AUTHOR OF THE plays *LOPSIDED* and *PANDORA'S GOLDEN BOX, and* the novels *Donning the Beard, The Second Heart, Soul Mistakes, Out of Grief,* and *Frankie & Petra*. EA is a Renaissance woman having worked in the theatre as an actor, director, and producer, and as a multi-media artist.

Other Plays by this Author

PANDORA'S GOLDEN BOX

A Musical

Conceived by Ellen Ann Kafkalas & Pamela Gould

Book and Lyrics by Ellen Ann Kafkalas

Music by David Pogue

This delightful musical for children follows the magical flight of Pandora, an orphan, into a world filled with turbulence and exotic characters. Pandora's adventurous fight against evil brings hers face-to-face with an important choice about the family she always wanted.

Synopsis

The Jones family is about to adopt a young girl from Greece, Pandora. Jason and Jennifer Jones are less than thrilled at the prospect of an additional sibling. Pandora is hesitant about meeting her new family but addresses her fears, "There's No Time For Fear," and then says goodbye to her chaperone and friend, Mrs. Croussouloudis. Mrs. Croussouloudis gives Pandora a golden box but tells her not to open it until she is in the right frame of mind.

At the Jones' residence, Pandora, Jason, and Jennifer are playing in Pandora's new room. Jason begins to make fun of Pandora's toys until he finds the box. When Pandora won't open the box for them, Jason tries but fails. Jason and Jennifer exit in a huff. They leave to spy on Pandora from a secret passageway. Alone in her room, Pandora dreams about running away, "If I Could Get Away," and opens the box. Once the box is opened there is a huge commotion—the real world disappears, and Pandora is sucked into the box.

In the fantasy world, servants are busy polishing spoons and shining mirrors. The evil queen, Hypodermia, who can turn them to stone with just one look, enslaves them. The servants wear protective eyewear to keep from being turned into stone. They are talking about their dreams and the power of dreams, "A Dream," when Hypodermia enters and threatens them if they don't keep working, "That's Why I'm the Queen." On a tirade, she rips their goggles off and turns them to stone. She leaves only her sisters, Sigh and Pester, alive to do the work.

Pandora lands in Olympia and is greeted by Clio, the main one's assistant, who briskly answers her questions and finishes her sentences. Chance Rival, adventurer, appears, and Clio sends the two of them off in search of Hypodermia's castle to capture Hypodermia and end her reign of terror. Clio advises them to find the Sisters of Rap, as they will have the answers of how to capture Hypodermia without being stoned. Chance explains to Pandora that Hypodermia was not always evil and that she fell under the spell of a magic potion, which she has become addicted to. Her addiction has ruined her and everything she touches.

In another part of Olympia, Jason and Jennifer appear. It is obvious that they have followed Pandora into the box, and they set out in search of her.

Chance and Pandora find the Sisters of Rap—Melody, Rhythm, and Rhyme—who share a boom box and a pair of sunglasses. All their speech is in the form of rap, and they can only see with the sunglasses, which they share. Chance asks the sisters to help. When they refuse, Pandora takes their sunglasses, and Chance takes their boom box. Paralyzed without their beat & sight, they tell Chance and Pandora to go off in search of the Nymphs of the West.

Chance and Pandora find the circle of light where the Nymphs—Vanity, Greed, and Ignorance reside. The Nymphs try to entice Pandora and Chance, "Into the Light," with promises of candy, cookies, toys, and riches. Pandora is seduced into the light and once inside, she realizes that it was all a trap. Chance tries to save her but must trade himself for the girl. Once inside the circle, Chance realizes that the Nymphs trapped him, and they are prisoners. Using the Nymphs' weakness against them, Pandora and Chance cause the Nymphs to break the circle and are free to go.

Hypodermia's sisters, Sigh and Pester, discuss their problem with Hypodermia, "The Hypodermia Blues." Pandora and Chance enter the castle courtyard. Their attempt to capture Hypodermia is successful, but in the attempt, Pandora is stoned. Jennifer and Jason catch up to Pandora just as she's turned to stone. Chance, Jason, Jennifer, Sigh, and Pester must join forces to help free Pandora from the spell. They set off in search of the Goddess of Love. On the way they encounter the three-headed dog, Bark, Snarl, and Ruff and must fight their way past the door, which guards the stairs to the goddess. The goddess tells them, "If You Got Love," you have the power to do anything. She tells them to look in their hearts and find what they love about Hypodermia. Back in the castle courtyard, Sigh and Pester begin to remember, and their love touches Hypodermia, breaking the spell. Once the spell is broken, Pandora is free. Pandora, Jason, and Jennifer return to the real world where they decide to get along as a family.

Made in the USA
Middletown, DE
27 October 2023

41347528R00057